Christ Be With Me

Adult Colouring Book

The Complete Text of the Christ Be with Me Prayer in Large, Simple Colouring Font with 14 Christian Cross Colouring Pages

ESTHER PINCINI

Christ Be with Me Adult Colouring Book
The Complete Text of the Christ Be with Me Prayer in Large, Simple Colouring Font
with 14 Christian Cross Colouring Pages

by Esther Pincini

Contains the full text of the original Christ Be with Me Prayer by St. Patrick

Creative Content Copyright © Magdalene Press 2017

ISBN 978-1-77335-030-1

No part of this publication may be reproduced, stored in a retrieval system,
or transmitted in any form or by any means, electronic, mechanical, photocopying,
recording or otherwise without written permission of the publisher.

Magdalene Press, 2017

Christ with me,

Christ before

me,

Christ behind me,

Christ

in

me,

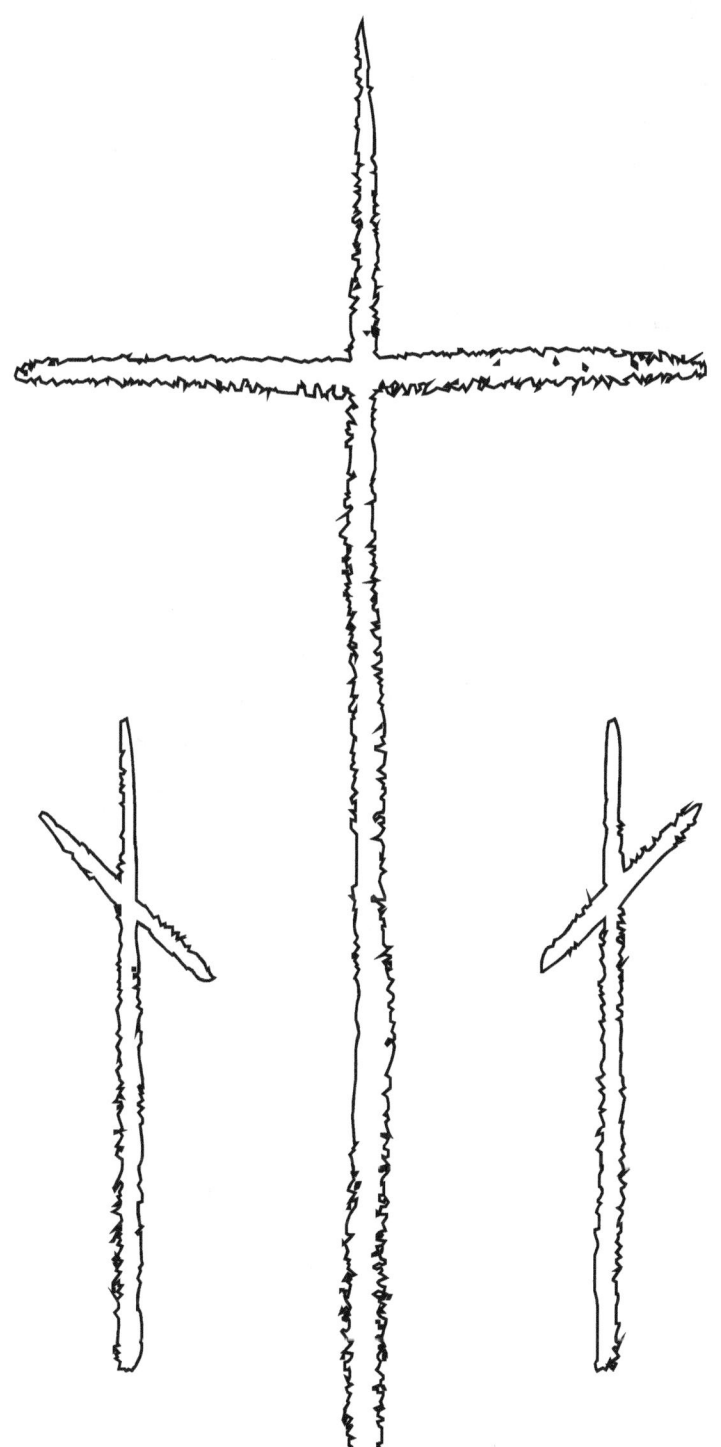

Christ beneath me,

Christ above me,

Christ on my right,

Christ on my left,

Christ where I lie,

Christ where I sit,

Christ where I arise,

Christ in the heart of

everyone who thinks of me,

Christ in the mouth of

every one who speaks to me,

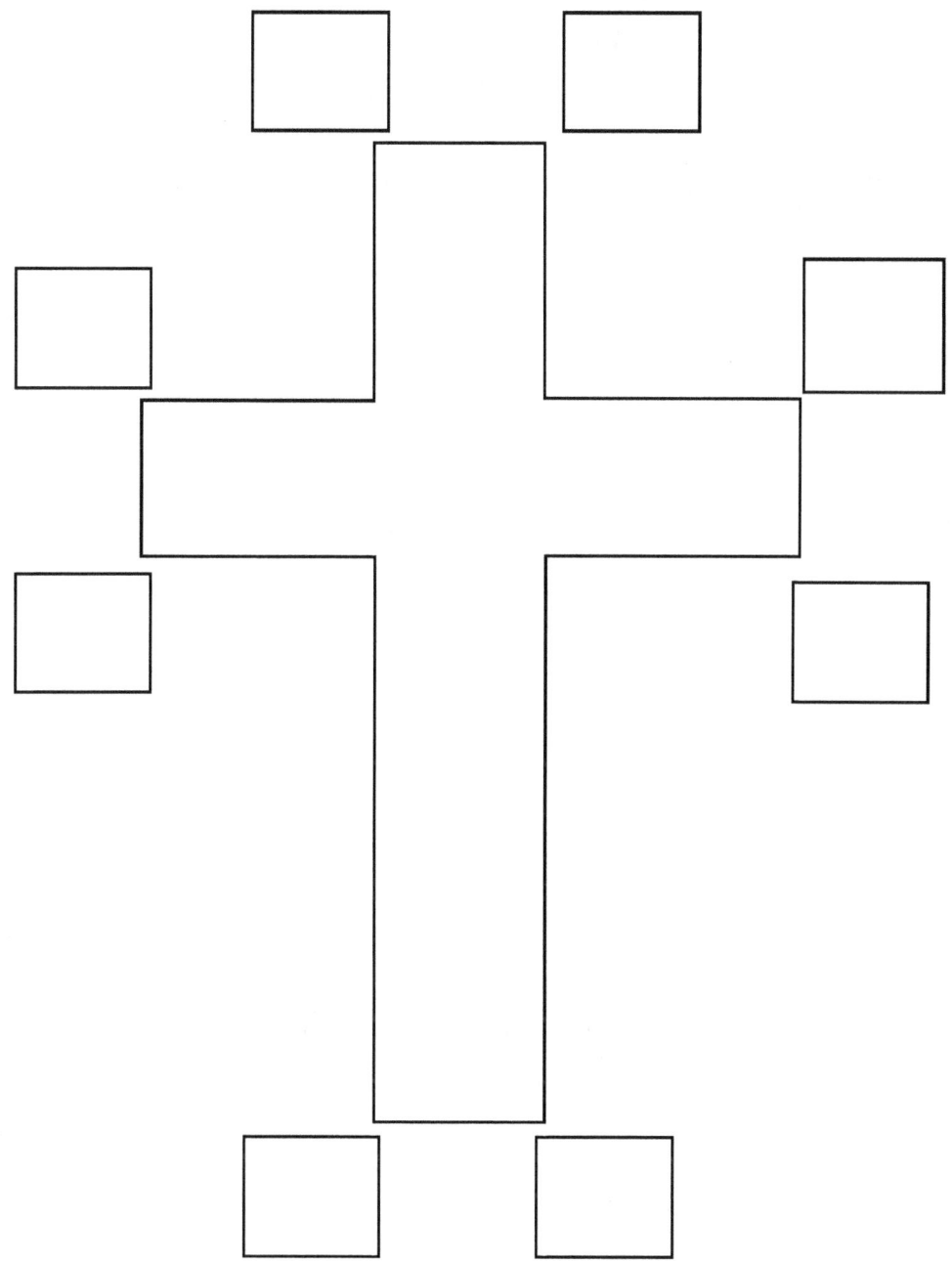

Christ in every eye

that

sees

me,

Christ in every ear

that
hears
me.

Salvation is of the Lord.

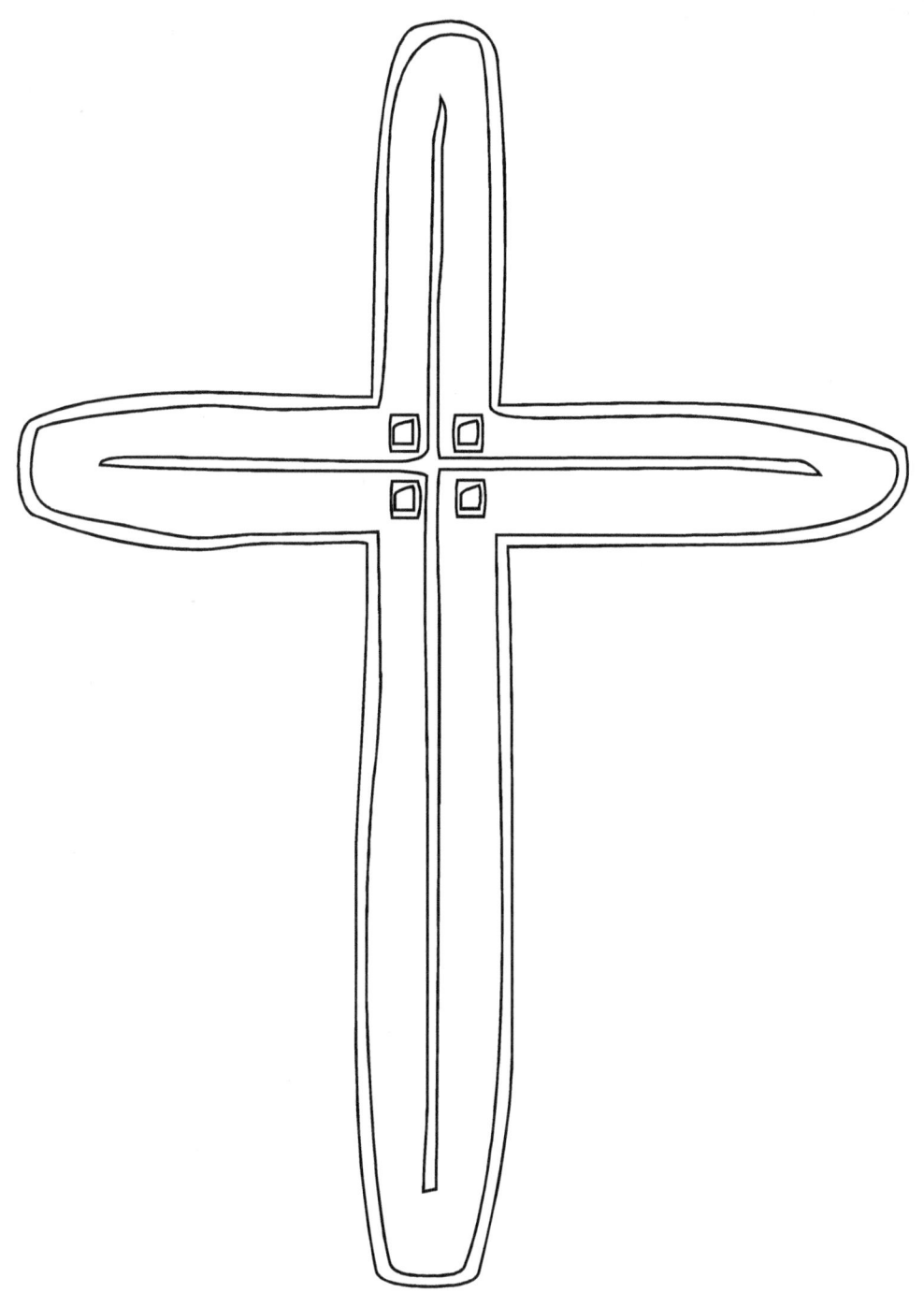

Salvation is of the Christ.

May your salvation,

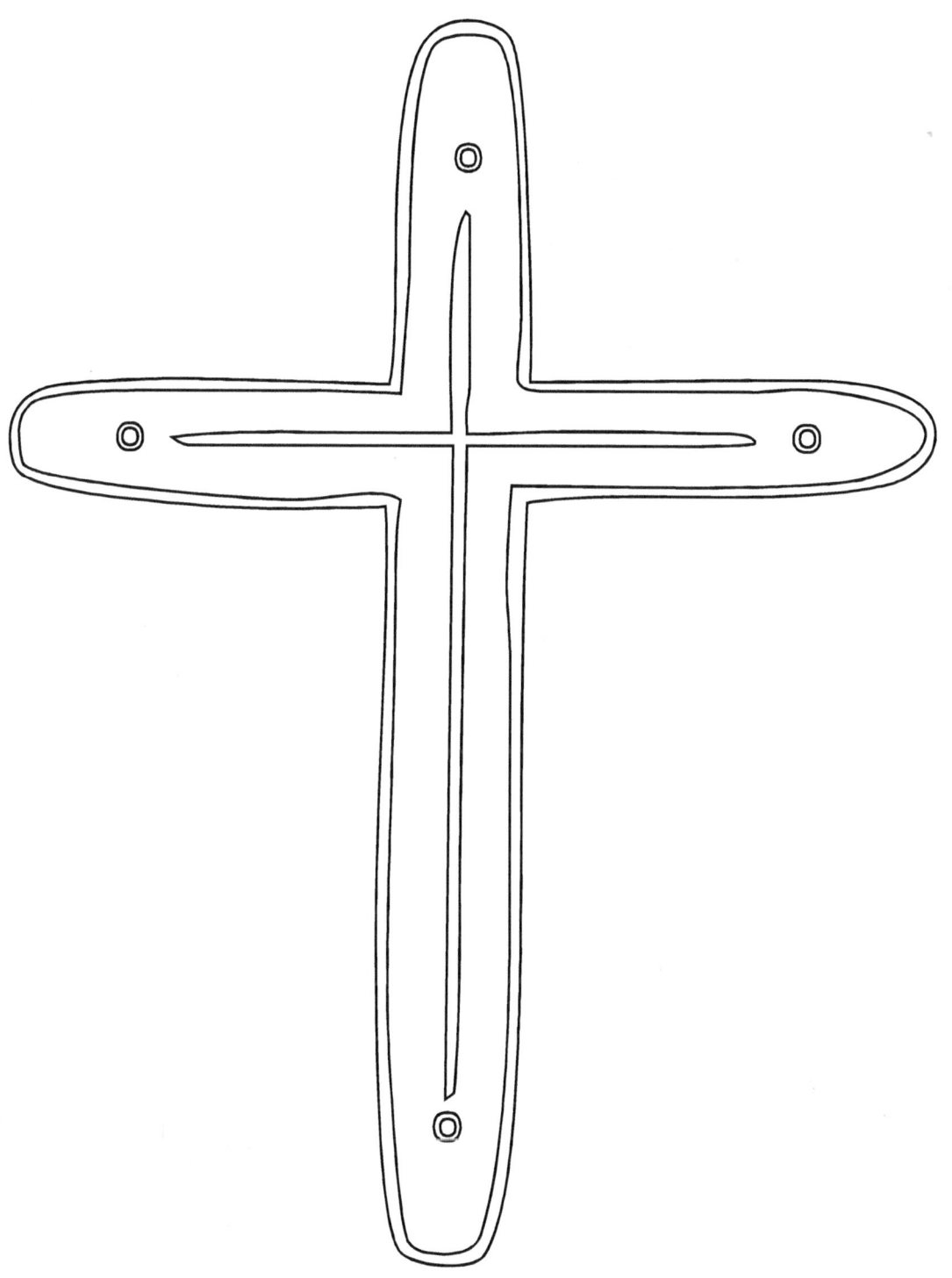

Lord, be ever with us.

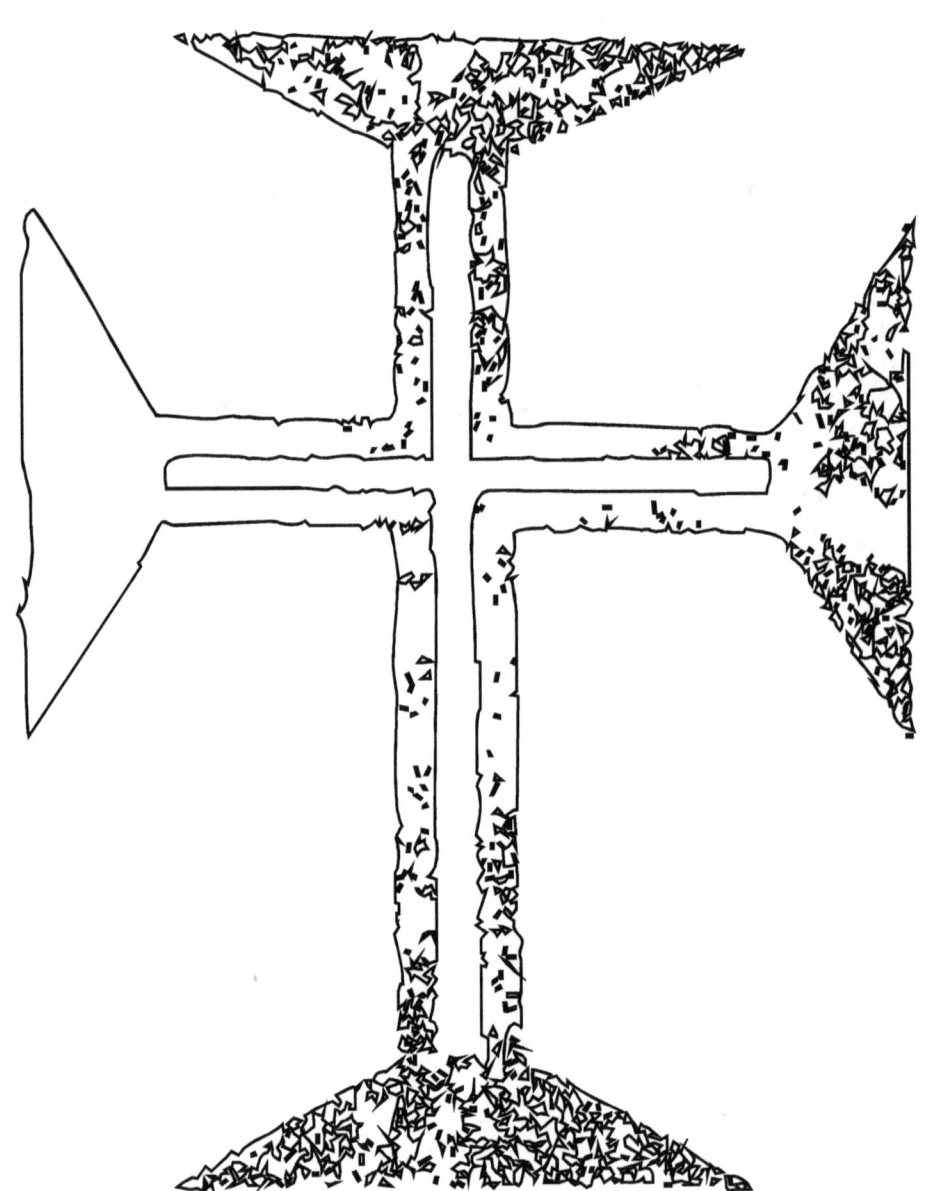

www.ingramcontent.com/pod-product-compliance
Lightning Source LLC
Chambersburg PA
CBHW081331040426

42453CB00013B/2381